Old Fort William
Guthrie Hutton

Looking south along High Street in 1936, with Cameron Square on the left and the Playhouse Cinema on the rig

Acknowledgements

Fort William is one of those places that has acted like a magnet and drawn me back on many occasions over a lifetime. I have sailed on the canal, run in the hills and tackled the joys of driving along High Street when it was the through road. Many of those memories flooded back as I trawled through research material and wandered the streets, looking for the stories to accompany the pictures in this little book, so thank-you Fort William, for just being there.

© Guthrie Hutton, 2015
First published in the United Kingdom, 2015, by Stenlake Publishing Ltd.
www.stenlake.co.uk
ISBN 9781840337006

The publishers regret that they cannot supply copies of any pictures featured in this book.

Further Reading

Cameron, A. D., *The Caledonian Canal*, (third edition) 1994.
Dow, Frances, *Cromwellian Scotland*, 1979 (reprinted 1999).
Gifford, John, *The Buildings of Scotland: Highlands and Islands*, 1992.
Grieves, Robert, *Wheels around Fort William and Lochaber*, 2003.
Haldane, A. R. B., *New Ways through the Glens*, 1962.
Company history, *History of the British Aluminium Company Limited: 1894 – 1955*.

Kilgour, Wm. T., *Twenty Years on Ben Nevis*, 1905, reprint 1985.
Maclean, Lorraine, *Discovering Inverness-shire*, 1988.
Martin, Paula, *Lochaber, A Historical Guide*, 2005.
Miers, Mary, *The Western Seaboard: An Illustrated Architectural Guide*, 2008.
Guidebook, *Mountain Moor and Loch*, 1895.
Thomas, John, *The West Highland Railway*, 1965.

Left: The sea level observatory in Fort William built to provide a comparative data set to the one taken at the observatory on the top of Ben Nevis.

Above: The proprietors of catering establishments on the summit of Ben Nevis put their stamp on postcards and other things as a form of advertising and as proof of their customer's adventure, but also perhaps, to deter light fingered souvenir hunters.

Introduction

Fort William is a hub where lochs, glens and rivers converge, but its growth was less dependent on these great natural advantages than on military developments. The first, Inverlochy Castle, was abandoned early in the fourteenth century leaving the area as little more than a meeting of the ways until, in the confusion of mid seventeenth century religion and politics, Oliver Cromwell rose to power in England and then extended his rule into Scotland.

Cromwell needed a military presence to impose his authority and suppress Royalist sympathies and so, after the Battle of Dunbar in 1650, his army pushed steadily up the east coast and into the southwest until it controlled most of the country south and east of the Highland glens. Wearied by years of war and religious disputes, Scots now paid higher taxes, but got something new in return: firm, fair government a measure of peace and some prosperity. Citadels were built to accommodate the army at Leith, Ayr, Perth and Inverness, but the Highlands still represented a potential source of trouble, so in June 1654 troops were brought over from Ireland to establish a new citadel at the strategically important location of Inverlochy. With Cromwell's death and the Restoration of the Monarchy the fort was abandoned, but thirty years later, King William's army built a new fort on the site and officials in Edinburgh named it after him. Local opinion of Fort William was quickly coloured by the part its troops played in the Massacre of Glencoe, but it remained in use for over 160 years.

A little town grew up adjacent to the fort and, in honour of William's wife, it was known as Maryburgh. Over the years, different landowners tried to replace her name with theirs, but almost perversely the name that stuck was none of these, but that of the fort that had been imposed on the area. Not even the Gaelic An Gearasdan, a reference to the garrison, rather than to the place it occupied, gained traction.

The fort had outlived its usefulness by the mid nineteenth century, but the site proved very useful when it became part of the infrastructure of the railway when it arrived in 1894. The railway transformed Fort William's fortunes, bringing an influx of tourists to fill the town's many new hotels. One of those hotels was even established on top of Ben Nevis alongside a remarkable, if short-lived, meteorological observatory.

Water pouring off Ben Nevis provided the principal ingredient for the town's main industry, distilling, but in the 1930s a water supply was driven though Ben Nevis in a tunnel to power a major new industry, the British Aluminium Company's Lochaber smelter. Another large industrial enterprise, a pulp and paper mill, was established at Corpach in the 1960s, but that did not last as long as the nearby Caledonian Canal, built in the first half of the nineteenth century. From Corpach the canal runs up through the Great Glen, where in the 1940s a remarkable experiment in cattle ranching was begun. It represented a new use for wild countryside that for some time had been given over to sheep or sporting estates. In more recent years sports of a different kind have attracted a range of enthusiasts to the hills and glens, making Fort William into a noted centre for outdoor activities. The town that scarcely existed when a troop of military men built their fort has grown into an activity hub worthy of its geographical position.

The old fort's inner gateway was removed in 1896 and re-erected at the entrance to Craigs Burial Ground.

Inverlochy Castle is the first known fortification to have been erected at the mouth of the River Lochy. It is thought to date from the thirteenth century, which makes it one of the oldest existing Scottish castles, albeit one that owes more to Norman influences than a native vernacular. It has a curtain wall enclosing a roughly square piece of ground, and circular towers at each corner, the largest of which is known as Comyn's Tower, a reference to the Comyn lords of Badenoch and Lochaber whose castle it was. Their tenure came to an abrupt and murderous end at the hands of Robert the Bruce and the castle was abandoned, a factor that contributed to its survival. It came back into use early in the sixteenth century when Alexander, second Earl of Huntly installed a garrison and the ancient walls acted as silent witness to two great battles fought nearby in 1431 and 1645. Early in the twentieth century the fourth Lord Abinger, attempted to enhance its antiquarian appeal by doing some repairs and making additions, but the old stonework has suffered more through time and exposure to West Highland weather.

Old Inverlochy Castle and the surrounding Torlundy Estate were bought in the 1830s by Sir James Scarlett, the first Baron Abinger, and on his death in 1844 passed to the second Baron, Robert Campbell Scarlett. William Frederick Scarlett, the third Baron Abinger, inherited the property in 1861, but not content with the housing arrangements of his forbears he engaged the architect, Robert Hesketh, to design a new mansion. Sited some two miles to the northeast of the old castle, but confusingly also named Inverlochy Castle, this great baronial pile was built between 1863 and 1866 and extended in the early 1890s. Jefferson Davis, the one and only president of the Confederate States of America, stayed at the house in 1869 and Queen Victoria visited in 1873, finding the situation 'lovely' and 'romantic'. The commandos, who used the house as a training base during the Second World War, may not have been so sentimental and they left both it and the grouse moors in such a poor state that the eighth Lord Abinger sold it all to whisky entrepreneur Joseph Hobbs. He died in 1963 and six years later the house was turned into an up market hotel.

The Inverlochy citadel established by the Cromwellian army was overlooked by high ground but partly surrounded by water and fronted by boggy land it had reasonable natural defences and, crucially for a fort in potentially hostile territory, it could be supplied by sea. The governor, Colonel Brayne, was given powers to impose law and order, acting as civil administrator and military enforcer. He left in 1656 and was followed in quick succession by two lieutenant colonels who in turn were superseded in 1657 by Major John Hill a man who combined the skills of a soldier with those of a diplomat, making him an ideal peacekeeper. Cromwell died in 1658, the Commonwealth ended and, with the Restoration of the Monarchy the fort was abandoned. Thirty years later, Protestantism was back in the ascendency, King James II had been ousted and William of Orange was on the throne. William's priorities were with France and Ireland and not wanting trouble from Highland Jacobites, he authorised General Mackay, the commander of his army in Scotland, to re-establish the Inverlochy fort (seen here in an engraving from 1848). In July 1690, less than two weeks after they started, the main body of soldiers departed, job done. The man left in charge was the now elderly Colonel John Hill.

Inverlochy Fort consisted of earth ramparts faced with stones taken from the river and loch. Its defences were strengthened with a ditch across the landward approach and cannon taken from the supply ships, much to the skippers' chagrin. As the military men set about their task of keeping a lid on Jacobitism, the little outpost was given its new name, Fort William, in honour of the king. Less honourably the fort was used as a base from which to mount the Massacre of Glencoe in February 1692, a tragedy that handed Jacobite propagandists an opportunity to foment unrest, which continued to simmer until it broke out in open rebellion in 1715 and again in 1745. An attack on the fort by Jacobite clansmen in March 1746 was repelled by the garrison, which then actively resisted a short siege. The incident prompted additional works, but with the Hanoverian monarchy entrenched and Jacobitism squashed the need for such a symbol of power became increasingly irrelevant. A garrison remained, latterly to chase smugglers, until 1854, after which the fort lay unused until it was sold.

This scene from 1905 of a train sitting at Fort William Station was repeated many times, with different engines and rolling stock, for nearly 100 years, but there was a time when people thought they would never see it. A couple of decades before the end of the nineteenth century townsfolk were worried that the lack of a railway was hampering progress. There was of course a steamer service from Oban, but after 1880 its timing could be affected by the late arrival there of the train from Glasgow. Another railway could be reached to the east at Dalwhinnie, but only after a long coach ride through the hills, on a rough bumpy road. Insult was added to injury by the knowledge that an earlier proposal to bring a railway through Glencoe had foundered, but the prayers were answered in August 1889 when the proposal to build the West Highland Railway was approved by parliament. Work got under way quickly, but the terrain over which the line was to be driven proved tough going and five more years elapsed before the line opened in August 1894.

Scotland's railway system was developed piecemeal by numerous small companies. Over time these were absorbed into larger operations and after a series of amalgamations in the 1860s two dominant players emerged, the North British Railway based in Edinburgh and Glasgow's Caledonian Railway. The 'Caley' regarded the west coast as its fiefdom, but to its chagrin the West Highland Railway was in partnership with the North British, which, from the start, was to be the operating company (it was quite common in the early days of railways for one company to build and manage the track and for another to run the trains). The locomotive seen in this picture arriving at Fort William Station (although the picture looks as if has been staged with a stationary train) was one of a class specially developed by the North British to haul moderately heavy trains at a gentle speed over the hills and round the bends of the West Highland. Based on an existing design, but with smaller driving wheels and shorter wheelbase, twelve of these engines were built for the opening of the line and another twelve were delivered in 1896.

Passengers on a train from Glasgow were in for a treat. Leaving behind the grime and smoke of the industrial city they glimpsed the Clyde Estuary, skirted Loch Lomond's bonny banks and gained height up Glen Falloch to Crianlarich. From there, still climbing and negotiating some engineering marvels like the horseshoe bend at the base of Ben Doran, the bleak magnificence of Rannoch Moor stretched ahead until descending past Loch Treig and Glen Spean they neared journey's end. And what an end it was, what a vista, as the hills opened out and the train rolled into town along the shore of Loch Linnhe, not from the south as logic might have dictated, but having looped around behind Ben Nevis, from the northeast. This lochside route represented a serious test for the people of Fort William of their enthusiasm for the railway, because the plans were well advanced before anyone realised the implications: that the rails would cut the town off from the shore. The track and its infrastructure can be seen squeezed into its narrow strip of ground, in this picture from April 1962, during the last days of steam on the West Highland line.

For a town intent on attracting visitors, a railway line acting as a barrier between the streets and the shore was a serious drawback, because it prevented development of a waterside promenade, the must-have tourist attraction of a Victorian resort. On its approach to the station the railway crossed the site of the old fort, which became the location of the sidings and locomotive sheds seen on the front cover of this book, and as if to emphasise the supplanting of infantry by industry, some of the old fort buildings became housing for railway employees. At the station, the single track main line fanned out into three platforms. The site was beside the pier, but somewhat cramped and occasionally, if outgoing trains were too long, they could effectively block the other platforms, while locomotives of extra-long incoming trains could impede road access to the pier, because the lochside track ran right through the station as is seen on the left of this picture from 1962. Once through the station the track continued across Station Square to a cargo-handling pier further south.

Fort William Station, on the left of this view looking from the pier to Gordon Square, was a curious architectural mixture. Built of red brick with stone facings and essentially conforming to the Arts & Crafts style popular at the time, it had a squat little tower redolent of a medieval keep and a pitched roof that projected like an awning. The station's location may have caused initial hand wringing, but while some in the town might have wished it had been on another site it was certainly convenient for steamer connections. Over time boats and trains were superseded as the principal means of travel by motor vehicles and Fort William's High Street became clogged with traffic, much of it just passing through on the way to somewhere else. The situation became so bad that, in order to divert traffic away from the town centre, a new bypass road was built along the loch shore using the route, and paradoxically perpetuating the barrier created by the railway. To make this happen, the station was closed and re-opened on a new site to the north of the town centre in June 1975.

A bus service between Fort William and North Ballachulish was begun by the North British Railway in 1906 and taken over after only a year by steamer operator David MacBrayne. It was the start of the company's extensive bus operations throughout the West Highlands and added significantly to Fort William's transport hub as this picture shows. The 1930s style building on the left was typical of MacBrayne's pier terminals at the time. Like the railway station it was demolished in the 1970s to make way for the new bypass road and the bus depot was relocated along with the station. The steamer coming alongside the pier, the *Lochfyne*, was built for David MacBrayne by Denny's Shipyard at Dumbarton and launched in March 1931. Unusually she was intended solely as a daytime passenger vessel with no cargo holds or sleeping accommodation, but more significantly she was the first British passenger vessel to be driven by diesel electric power. Such was the interest in her in the great shipbuilding centre of Glasgow that she was exhibited to the public before entering service. She came onto the Fort William run in 1936.

St Mary's Roman Catholic Church, seen here at the head of Gordon Square in a view looking from Station Square, was erected in 1868. It remained a place of worship until 1923 after which it became a garage belonging to Inverness-based automotive dealer and bus operator, MacRae & Dick. The company was involved in a dramatic incident in 1928 when one of their charabancs started to move without a driver. Two women on board managed to jump off as the bus gathered speed. It rolled across High Street into Station Square and was heading for the loch when, by good fortune, it collided with the pier office and rebounded onto one of MacBrayne's vehicles, which brought it to a halt. MacRae & Dick were not the first transport undertaking to operate from Gordon Square. They were preceded by an early bus operator, A. & J. MacPherson, and before them by MacGregor & Cameron who hired horses. The sign for their 'posting establishment' can be seen to the right of St. Mary's.

Sitting on the hillside above Gordon Square, in the picture on the facing page, is the Station Hotel. Built in 1895 to the designs of architect Duncan Cameron it was typical of the grand hotels erected to cater for wealthy rail passengers. It was later renamed the Highland Hotel and was for a time owned by the Polytechnic Touring Association, the forerunner of Lunn Poly, which later became Thomson Holidays. It was taken over during the Second World War by the Royal Navy, which used it as a base for HMS St Christopher, a coastal forces training establishment. A number of other hotels and private houses in the town were used to accommodate naval personnel, one of which was the Grand, which occupied the northern corner of Gordon Square with High Street. Situated on the opposite corner was the Waverley Hotel, seen here in a picture from about 1905. It was a temperance hotel, one of a number in the town catering for people at a time of heightened concern about the malign effects of the demon drink.

Another of Fort William's catering establishments was the West End Hotel seen to the left of this picture from the early 1920s. Many of the late nineteenth and early twentieth century hotels have either gone or changed their name, but the West End, with spectacular views and close proximity to the town, not only survived, but expanded by taking over the site of the neighbouring house. In front of the hotel, the little bit of loch shore that the railway left for townspeople to enjoy, appears to be something of a playground for youngsters, although it has since been turned into a car park. Above and beyond the beach is Achintore Road, characterised by a string of fine villas and one significant public building. In the centre of the picture is the former manse of the United Free Church and beyond that, the building with the little spire, was the Kilmallie School Board's public school, built in 1876 in response to the Education Act of 1872, which made education compulsory for all children between the ages of five and thirteen.

As motor traffic grew through the twentieth century, Achintore Road grew with it, with houses, hotels and guest houses, eventually stretching for over two miles to the south of the town centre. The views across the loch to the hills of Ardgour are special, so the attraction is obvious, as it presumably was for the campers and caravanners who used this little site, known as Woodlands. It is not known when the picture was taken, but the vehicles and tents suggest a date around the late 1940s or early 1950s. The site appears to have few facilities, the caravans look basic and the tents have an 'army surplus' look about them, but in those austere post-war years people were just happy to get out into the great outdoors. Wind and rain were just part of the experience, but so too according to a camping enthusiast writing in 1955, were 'friendly conversations with local farmers and fellow campers, and the sense of satisfaction and wellbeing that always comes from a long spell under canvas'. Hmm!

High Street, seen here in a picture looking north from the junction with Gordon and Station Squares, formed part of the A82, the main road between Glasgow and Inverness. There is not much traffic, but as this increased, so did the congestion eventually leading to this section of the street being pedestrianized. Prominent to the right of the picture is Fraser's Café & Restaurant, which was a feature of High Street from the 1920s until the 1970s when it became the popular restaurant and nightclub, McTavish's Kitchen. The two restaurants held many happy memories for local people and visitors alike, but these were snuffed out in June 2006 when the building was gutted by a major fire that also destroyed the neighbouring travel business and the Gift Box, seen in this picture as the Gift Shop. Across the street is one of Fort William's more distinctive buildings, the half-timbered and harled Queen Anne House. Its twin gables to the front can just be seen to the left of centre.

High Street is seen here, a little to the north of the picture on the facing page. The most prominent feature is the large and imposing Palace Hotel, which is displaying an AA sign, a sure indication of its status as a well-regarded establishment. It has since been renamed Ossian's. Hotels in urban centres often had shops occupying the ground floor and a stair leading up to a first floor reception. R. S. McColl, on the left, was one of a chain of newsagents and confectioners founded in 1901 by Robert Smyth McColl, a former professional footballer from Glasgow. Beyond the Palace Hotel is Fort William's former palace of entertainment, the Playhouse Cinema. Designed to accommodate 678 customers it was built in the early 1930s by Cowiesons Ltd., a structural engineering company from Glasgow, but in common with many other cinemas, the Playhouse succumbed to the challenge of television, closing in 1978. The building was used for a time as a bingo club and then demolished.

Initially known as the 79th regiment of foot, the Queen's Own Cameron Highlanders was raised at Fort William in 1793 by Major Alan Cameron of Erracht. When the First World War broke out the regiment consisted of two battalions and with more men urgently needed Sir Donald Cameron of Lochiel, the 25th chief of the clan, raised a new 5th Battalion with himself in command. Known as 'Lochiel's Own', they formed part of the 9th (Scottish) Division, which took part in the Battle of Loos in September/October 1915. At a battle within the battle, at Hohenzollern Redoubt, the battalion sustained heavy casualties, but for his part in the action, Corporal James Dalgleish Pollock, was awarded a Victoria Cross. After the war the army slimmed down to a peacetime size and in 1921, during the anniversary of the Battle of Loos, the colours of 'Lochiel's Own' were laid up in Fort William town hall in Cameron Square. Led by a piper a colour party consisting of former men of the 5th Battalion, a detachment from Cameron Barracks in Inverness and members of the local Territorial company of the 4th Battalion, marched along High Street from the Craigs and formed up in the square, where Lochiel is seen receiving the colour from Lieutenant Weir.

Continuing the story from the facing page, Lochiel is seen handing the colour to Provost Stewart outside the town hall. Accompanied by members of the town council, the provost took the colour into the hall where a ceremony was held to accept it on behalf of the town. At the time this ceremony took place the town hall was a focal point for Cameron Square and the civic centre of Fort William. Originally erected as a church in the late eighteenth century, the building was reused as another church when the first one closed in the mid nineteenth century and was then adapted for its civic role, opening in 1881. Fort William lost its burgh status as a result of local government reorganisation in 1975 and as if registering a silent protest, the hall went up in flames in December of that year. Despite the loss of the hall, Cameron Square remained a focal point for the town as the location of the West Highland Museum, which opened in 1923. It holds a fine collection of local and Jacobite memorabilia, including panelling from the former governor's office at the fort where a heavy-hearted Colonel Hill signed the order for the Massacre of Glencoe.

Fort William's congested High Street was the cause of much irritation for drivers trying to get from one end to the other, so a clear road, such as the one seen in this picture, would have answered many prayers. Pedestrians may have taken a contrary view as they jostled for space on the crowded footpaths. They are wrapped up against the weather and with the surface of the road looking wet, the photographer has, perhaps unwittingly, reinforced the town's reputation for rain. The picture, undated but probably taken around 1960, looks south from a point near Fraser Square and illustrates the High Street's wide variety of shops. On the right, in what was the ground floor of the Argyll Hotel building, is The Fruit Bazaar, which also sold flowers, then licensed grocer D. & J. MacEwen, ironmonger Marshall & Pearson and beyond their shop a chemist that later became Boots, a shoe shop and many more. The two vehicles parked nearest to camera were probably local because they are displaying the Inverness-shire registration letters, ST.

Motor vehicles had evidently begun to make their presence felt on High Street by the early 1920s when this picture was taken looking south from the junction with Fraser Square. Horses are not in evidence, but on the right is a distinctive circular trough and lamp standard, a match to the one seen on page 14 at the top of Station Square, which suggests that Fort William's streets were once busy with horse-drawn traffic. The building on the extreme left of the picture was erected in 1911 for the National Bank of Scotland. In 1958 it became a branch of the National Commercial Bank, which merged with the Royal Bank of Scotland in 1969. The buildings to the right of the bank have since been replaced by modern shops and the pedestrianized road surfaced with cobbles and slabs and furnished with a variety of bollards, benches, bike racks and other objects. With the introduction of such measures pedestrians could wander at will – which they seem to have been doing quite happily in the 1920s, while taking care to carry that ever-handy accessory, an umbrella.

The railway may have enhanced Fort William's prospects of realising its potential as a tourist destination, but to capitalise fully on its natural advantages it needed places for people to stay. In those early days, hotels were mainly located in the town centre, many along High Street, and those that were at a little distance collected passengers from trains and steamers in their own horse-drawn buses and conveyed them to their accommodation. One town centre hotel was the Imperial, bounded on three sides by Fraser Square, Middle Street and Low Street (on the right). The railway line ran alongside Low Street, so the photographer who took this picture in the 1950s has turned their back on it and excluded what might have been regarded as a less than appealing prospect. Since the picture was taken some High Street hotels have closed, but the Imperial bucked the trend, its former back-street situation enhanced by the removal of the railway and changes to traffic arrangements through the town.

Retail co-operative societies usually grew out of industrial communities, but with few of these in the Highlands, there was only a scattering of co-ops in the north and west. Fort William provided an exception when the Lochaber and District Co-operative Society opened in 1918. A railway carriage, seen behind the store on the right, is a pointer to the industrial base from which it will have drawn many members. One of the largest retail outlets in the town, the store also spawned branches at Banavie, Annat and Arisaig, all places situated on the West Highland Railway's Mallaig extension. The Fort William Co-op provided a wide range of goods and services: groceries of course, but also bread, meat, boots and shoes, clothing and, as technology advanced, radios and televisions. The local society remained in existence until 1969 when the Scottish Co-operative Wholesale Society (SCWS) took over. It had been SCWS policy for over half a century to open stores in places where none existed and by taking over in Fort William they ensured that the Co-op name would continue and expand into other local areas like Caol.

The word 'parade' is often used to give a street name some cache, but at Fort William 'The Parade' is simply a shortened description of what was once the old fort's parade ground. It is seen here in 1950, with the Duncansburgh Parish Church flanked on the right by the 1930s manse, and on the left by the Alexandra Hotel. Dating from 1876, the hotel was always one of the town's more up market establishments, recommended to their members by prestigious motoring organisations and marketed as the 'nearest hotel to Ben Nevis'. Fort William is situated in Kilmallie Parish, but with the parish church at Corpach and a large number of parishioners in 'the Fort', a subsidiary, or 'quoad sacra', ecclesiastical parish was established in July 1860, and the church erected to provide a suitable place of worship in 1881. The congregation amalgamated with that of the Macintosh Memorial Church, from Fassifern Road, in 2007. In front of the church is a large statue erected in 1909 to commemorate Donald Cameron of Lochiel, the 24th chief of Clan Cameron. To its left is the town's war memorial, one of a number of memorials situated on The Parade.

Tucked in behind The Parade was the large and imposing Invernevis House, home of the distillery owning Macdonald family. The first of the family's distilleries was the Ben Nevis, built in 1825 by 'Long John' Macdonald. It was situated about two miles out of Fort William, close to Inverlochy Castle where Mr. Macdonald kept a herd of cattle fed on used grains from the distillery. John Macdonald died in 1856 leaving his son Donald P. MacDonald in charge of the business. He expanded the output of the old distillery and in 1878 built the new Nevis Distillery on six acres of ground near the mouth of the River Nevis. When Donald P. died in 1891, the business passed to his sons and was eventually sold in 1941 to Joseph Hobbs. The family's town estates, including Invernevis House, were bequeathed to the Catholic parish in 1925. The house initially became a convent for the Sisters of Charity and then the Sisters of Notre Dame who taught at Saint Mary's School until the late 1950s after which the house and land were sold for the building of the new Belford Hospital.

One of Fort William's most cherished institutions, Belford Hospital is also one of the best known featuring regularly on national news media when things go wrong in the mountains. The original hospital, seen here in a picture from about 1905, was on the other side of the road, a bit further out of town. It was built in 1863 by estate factor and lawyer, Andrew Belford, who donated it to Kilmallie and Kilmonivaig parishes. It had a total of 30 beds in two main wards and some smaller rooms. In those pre-NHS days, money had to be raised through events like the public appeal that raised over £1,500 to fund a new operating theatre, which was opened in 1927 by the Duke of York, the future King George VI. His daughter, Princess Margaret, opened the new Belford Hospital in April 1965, but not without a little drama. The previous day, three 45 ton aluminium waggons jumped the rails just outside Fort William and despite frantic efforts to clear the line it was decided not to risk the Royal Train and instead of arriving at the station, the princess came by car from Spean Bridge.

It was not easy to be a Catholic following the Reformation of 1560, but despite restrictions on worship that lasted for over 200 years many people in Lochaber held firm to the old church. With official attitudes easing in the late eighteenth century a mission church was established in what became Gordon Square. This was replaced in 1867 by St. Mary's Church, which also had a small school attached. Both church and school were judged to be inadequate by William MacMaster, a new priest who arrived in 1922. Helped by the bequest to the parish of the MacDonald town estates he raised the money to build a new school, which opened in February 1932. The fund-raising then went into overdrive and designs for a new St. Mary's Church, which featured a massive tower as a dramatic main feature, were prepared by Edinburgh architect Reginald Fairlie. Situated beside Belford Road, the foundation stone was laid in June 1933 and the new church was opened and consecrated by Bishop Martin of Argyll and the Isles in October 1934.

FORT WILLIAM GAMES, GRAND STAND

With women in frocks and bonnets, and men in tweeds and suits, a goodly throng has crowded onto what the title of this picture describes as the Fort William Games Grandstand. The picture is undated, but must have been taken at some time between 1903 and 1914 when local man Alexander Anthony Cameron was a Highland Games heavyweight champion, competing at events throughout the country. Fort William has always had a fondness for the games of the Gael, including shinty, and indeed the men of Brae Lochaber are credited with introducing a leather-cased ball to replace the old style ball, made of hair. Lowland sporting imports have also proved popular, especially football, but in recent years people have been attracted to the area to climb up the mountains or speed down them on skis or mountain bikes. The town has also been the destination for legions of long distance walkers tackling the West Highland Way, and all this activity has resulted in the area marketing itself as an 'outdoor capital', no mean feat for a place with high rainfall.

With the River Nevis curling in on the left, Inverlochy in the centre and the River Lochy running across from right to left, this picture looks north-west from the slopes of Cow Hill to Corpach in the distance. In the foreground is the Glennevis Distillery, a relatively small-scale operation that made whisky for blending. Started up in 1901, it was stopped in 1917, along with other distilleries, when the wartime government decided that barley should be used for food, not making whisky. Under new owners it started up again in the 1920s and in the 1930s was bought by a Glasgow company, Train & McIntyre, which ran its operations through a distilling subsidiary, Associated Scottish Distilleries. The driving force in these operations was Joseph Hobbs, a man who would stamp his personality all over Lochaber. He later bought the Ben Nevis and Nevis distilleries; part of the latter can be seen on the extreme left of the picture. Glenlochy was sold to the Distillers Company Limited in 1953 and managed by their subsidiary Scottish Malt Distilleries for thirty years until they decided it was surplus to requirements and closed it down. Some of the distillery houses were turned into a guesthouse and the malt barns became flats.

Inverlochy is seen here looking from Montrose Square to Wades Road in August 1930. The village was built as part of the Lochaber smelter development of the British Aluminium Company (BAC). The company came into existence in 1894 after a way was discovered to isolate alumina and then, using electrolysis, extract the metal. The process needed huge quantities of cheap reliable power and although untried on the scale required and still in its infancy, hydro-electricity was the best option, and the best place to establish the generating infrastructure was the West Highlands. The first smelter was built at Foyers beside Loch Ness, but its capacity for expansion was limited, so the company set about building the Blackwater Dam to impound a huge new reservoir to supply a generating station and factory at the head of Loch Leven. Work on the dam and water supply system began in 1905 and the Kinlochleven smelter went into production in February 1909. The First World War and the years that followed saw demand for aluminium grow rapidly, prompting the BAC to seek further expansion. The result was the Lochaber smelter.

The British Aluminium Company's original plan was to divert water from a large catchment area into Loch Treig and then, by tunnelling through the intervening hills, feed it to Kinlochleven. The plan hit a snag: Inverness County Council objected to water from their county being diverted into Argyll so the company had to modify the scheme. It was passed through parliament in 1921 and construction began in 1924. Canteens and accommodation huts for 2,000 men were erected, a temporary power station was built and over twenty miles of narrow gauge railway tracks were laid, all as preliminaries to the main element of the job, a fifteen-mile long, concrete-lined tunnel through Ben Nevis from Loch Treig. With the tunnel complete, pipelines laid on the face of Ben Nevis and a 2,000 feet long reinforced concrete jetty built out into Loch Linnhe, the new smelter went in operation at the end of 1929. That was only the start and in 1931 work began on the next phase of the development, which included construction of the spectacular Loch Laggan Dam, seen here in its early stages.

As well as building the impressive Laggan Dam, a three-mile long tunnel had to be cut to run water from Loch Laggan into Loch Treig where a 700 feet long dam, made of earth with a concrete core raised the level of the loch by 35 feet. This was enough to flood the West Highland Railway line, so a mile and half of track, 150 yards of which was driven through a new tunnel, was re-laid at a higher level. The little train hauled by a Sentinel steam engine and seen here delivering a party of dignitaries to a ceremony at the Loch Treig dam was not on the main line, but on the three-foot gauge track used by the contractor, Balfour Beatty. They completed the combined Loch Laggan, Loch Treig scheme in 1938, increasing the volume of water and allowing the power station and works at Fort William to be extended. In a third element of the project, carried out during the Second World War with the assistance of Canadian soldiers, River Spey floodwaters were diverted into Loch Laggan.

The men carving a hole through Ben Nevis lived in twelve hutted camps on the mountainside and were supplied by daily canteen and mail trains. It was a hard job in a tough environment (although tunnellers tend to describe their work as boring - think about it!), but it was finite, whereas people employed at the smelter were expected to be there for a while, so some 300 houses were built at Inverlochy. Although the company was involved in the process, the development was carried out by the Inverlochy Village Society Ltd, a co-operative housing structure modelled on a similar one that had taken over housing provision in Kinlochleven. Inverness County Council built some of the houses at Inverlochy and the village also contained a post office, shops, a children's playground and village hall. It is seen here in August 1930, in a view looking up Montrose Avenue with the company's estate offices just to the left of centre. Everything looks raw and new, with immature trees in protective cages, telegraph poles and ground still recovering from the impact of building work.

Speaking in Glasgow in September 1930, Labour politician George Lansbury outlined a vision of a network of 'hostels for hikers' set up around the country. The idea struck a chord and the following year, at a meeting in Edinburgh, the Scottish Youth Hostels Association (SYHA) was formed. The hostels were to have dormitories, shared living spaces and communal cooking facilities, and hostellers would be expected to 'muck in' to do the chores. The first hostel was set up near Yarrow in the Borders, one of nine in the first year offering a total of 227 beds. Six hostels were added in 1932 and seventeen more in 1933, including a small one in Glen Nevis. The glen, with its proximity to the great hill-walking country of the Mamores and Ben Nevis, was so highly regarded that the hostel had no sooner opened than it was unable to meet demand and so a bigger hostel was built. The first in Scotland to use Norwegian timber construction, it was opened in July 1938 by Commander Adams, secretary of the King George's Jubilee Trust, which provided grant funding. With accommodation for 133, the new Glen Nevis hostel was one of the SYHA's largest at that time.

For hikers and hostellers, Glen Nevis was a gateway to glorious mountain terrain, but for many Victorian and Edwardian tourists who had arrived in Fort William by boat or train the hills were best viewed from afar, or the comfort of a coach. Coach tours were popular and people had a number of options, at Glenfinnan they could see where Bonnie Prince Charlie raised his standard in 1745, head up to the 'Dark Mile' at Achnacarry or they could take the shorter, but arguably more attractive trip up Glen Nevis to the road end at Achriabhach, seen here in an Edwardian era picture. A contemporary guidebook described the glen as 'very wild and picturesque . . . threaded by the crystal waters of the River Nevis', and it singled out the waterfalls, including those 'foaming down the side of Ben Nevis', for special mention. The 'rocking stone', a large mass of mica slate, was labelled as 'Druidical', which added the enticement of mystery to a natural wonder. Antiquity, which also fascinated, came in the handy form of Dun Deardail, the vitrified fort on the west side of the glen. But in reality no tourist industry hyperbole was necessary, because the attractions of Glen Nevis needed (still need) no exaggeration. For a few, however, there is the opportunity to experience the attractions in an entirely different way. Since 1973 (with a gap between 2003 and 2008) a two mile stretch of the river has hosted the Glen Nevis Air Bed Race. The competitors brave the water, icy cold even in July, the waterfalls and the features of the river with names like 'Dead Dog Pool' and 'The Leg Breaker'. The madness is all in a good cause and the proceeds of the event support the Lochaber Mountain Rescue.

Ben Nevis was a nineteenth century meteorologist's dream. It was the highest mountain in the British Isles, fully exposed to the elements and in the path of weather systems as they rolled in unimpeded from the west. The dream was to gather data on the summit and a proposal to do this was put forward in the 1870s. It failed to garner support, but in 1881 a man named Clement Wragge (and nicknamed Inclement Wragge) set about the task. Leaving his home before 5 o'clock every morning, from the start of June to mid October, he trekked to the summit, taking readings at set locations as he went. While he made his observations, his wife Leonora took readings in Fort William for comparison. Helped by a couple of assistants Wragge did the same work the following two years, demonstrating that automatic instruments could not be relied on in the harsh conditions and giving the Scottish Meteorological Society the ammunition it needed to raise the money to build a permanent observatory. It was opened in October 1883, manned by a superintendent and two assistants, but despite his efforts, Clement Wragge was not one of them. He migrated to Australia; it was warmer there.

The meteorologists at the summit endured very harsh conditions: winds that blew them off their feet, rain that froze on contact and snow that cocooned the observatory, but the data they collected so impressed the scientific community that the Edinburgh International Exhibition of 1886 presented the Scottish Meteorological Society with £1,000. The society used this windfall to expand their activities by building a sea-level observatory. It was situated in Achintore Road and completed in 1890 (see page 2). The picture shows the observatory with a new neighbour, a hotel, which opened in 1894, the year the West Highland Railway arrived in town. It was not of course a five-star establishment, but did provide overnight accommodation for anyone who wanted to boast that they had spent the night on top of the Ben, although they could not immediately toast their achievement because it was a temperance hotel. Constantly dogged by a lack of money the observatory closed in 1904, but the hotel and refreshment room kept going, even incorporating part of the old observatory before closing in 1916.

With a path having been created to get to and from the observatory, it was inevitable that people other than scientists and tourists would want to use it to get to the top. In May 1911, with motoring in its infancy, Henry Alexander set out to conquer the mountain in a car. His father owned the main Ford dealership in Edinburgh, so unsurprisingly he chose a Model T Ford for this feat. It took three days to get to the summit, with a team of horses provided by A. & J. MacPherson of Gordon Square in attendance, but generally not included in photographs. The car stayed on the mountain overnight before descending in a mere two and half hours the following day. That return journey was followed by a triumphal parade through the streets of Fort William and a civic reception – due reward for generating publicity for the town's tourist trade, Ford cars and Dunlop tyres. Seventeen years later Henry Alexander repeated his adventure, this time in a new Model A Ford, and since then a number of other car and motor bike enthusiasts have powered their way to the top.

Flowing out of Loch Lochy, and combined with the waters of the River Spean, the River Lochy was a formidable barrier to travellers and drovers. The only crossing was a ferry, which a mid nineteenth century account described as 'excellent', with 'good quays' on either side, but nevertheless regarded it as a poor substitute for a bridge. It was clearly not an isolated opinion, because the ferry was soon replaced by a suspension bridge. That elegant structure was itself superseded in the late 1920s by a bridge supported on reinforced concrete columns. Designed by Sir E. Owen Williams with architectural input from Maxwell Ayrton, it is seen here with the Ben Nevis Distillery, on the east bank of the river, artfully framed in the stone arch. The arches at each end originally held the suspension cables for the earlier bridge, but were retained when it was rebuilt. Wide enough for only single track road the bridge was replaced with one of three lanes width, to coincide with the building of the pulp and paper mill at Corpach.

Joseph W. Hobbs was born in Britain, but brought up in Canada where he made a fortune, and then lost it during the great depression. Reinventing himself, he arrived in Scotland and became a whisky entrepreneur with such success he was able to buy Inverlochy Castle and Estate in 1946. Looking around at his new land holdings he saw another business opportunity and, drawing on his Canadian background, turned 10,000 acres of formerly unproductive land into the Great Glen Cattle Ranch. Using land in the Scottish Highlands as a cattle ranch was certainly different to running sheep or pursuing wildlife. This remarkable venture started with 70 beef cattle, but the herd soon numbered over 1,000 animals. Seven hundred acres of ground were sown with crops to provide silage for winter-feed. A number of concrete animal shelters gave people travelling on the A82 road something surprising and new to look at. One of them is seen here with cattle being herded in by the local rancheros, mounted on sturdy Highland ponies.

The arrival of southern soldiery in their fiefdom was not exactly welcomed by Clan Cameron and clan chief, Sir Ewan Cameron, put a little distance between himself and them by moving north from Torcastle, beside the River Lochy, to the banks of the River Arkaig at Achnacarry. It was a name that became closely associated with Jacobitism and it is possible that Bonnie Prince Charlie's uprising could have faltered had it not been for the support of the 'Gentle Lochiel'. The clan suffered for that support and following the Battle of Culloden the estate was forfeited, and then recovered for the family in 1784, when Donald Cameron, the 22nd chief, paid the fine. Some years later, a new Achnacarry House was built to the designs of architect James Gillespie Graham. The building was begun in 1802, but not fully finished until the 1830s. It is seen here behind a gathering of people who have congregated for a garden party to celebrate the laying of the foundation stone of the new St. Ciaran's Church, completed in 1911.

A branch railway line, opened on 1st June 1895, went from Fort William across the River Lochy and terminated at Banavie, beside the Caledonian Canal. Goods wagons could be shunted back and forth up a steep gradient to the canal bank, but the station was on a lower level. Passengers travelling by canal steamer to Inverness and all points in between had to climb up to Banavie Pier, situated at the top of the lock-flight known as Neptune's Staircase. That seems to be the subject of this picture, passengers walking toward the *Gondolier*, while a piper busks for their entertainment and a wee boy in a big coat holds out his cap for money. Built in 1866 *Gondolier* was the best-known steamer on the route, but for many years she ran daily in tandem with another vessel, the one going south while the other went north and passing in the middle, usually on Loch Oich. The first consort on the route, *Glengarry*, was replaced when the railway opened in 1895 by *Gairlochy*, but she was burned to the waterline at Fort Augustus on Christmas Eve 1919. *Gondolier* carried on, working the route on her own until she was withdrawn in 1939.

The maintenance boat in this picture from 1962 is seen through the open deck of the swing bridge at the foot of Neptune's Staircase. Originally the road crossed the canal on a double leaf swing bridge that spanned one of the lock chambers halfway up the flight. That bridge was replaced in the early 1930s by the one seen here, built by the Glasgow engineering firm of Sir William Arrol. Like the Lochy Bridge, it was only wide enough for a single track road so, shortly after this picture was taken, with the Corpach pulp and paper mill generating increased traffic, a new swing bridge of two carriageways width was installed. Beyond the road bridge is the lattice girder swing bridge built to carry the Mallaig railway across the canal. The promoters of the West Highland Railway had always intended to terminate their line at a point on the coast where a fishing port could be developed, but met determined opposition before gaining parliamentary approval. Construction began with Lady Margaret Cameron of Lochiel cutting the first sod at Corpach on 21st January 1897. The line was completed in time for the first train to run in April 1901.

The Caledonian Canal is one of the country's most impressive structures. Linking Lochs Lochy, Oich and Ness with man-made channels, it stretches for over 60 miles through the Great Glen from Inverness in the north and east, to Corpach in the south and west. It was one of the first major nationalised transport undertakings, commissioned by the government as a way of providing work in the Highlands to stem the flow of emigration. Designed by the great Scottish civil engineer, Thomas Telford, construction and excavation work began in 1803, with the basin at Corpach proving to be one of the most demanding tasks, because the navvies had to hack it out of solid rock with hand tools. A pair of staircase locks was built at the Banavie end of the basin while at the other end was the all-important sea-lock, connecting the canal to salt water. Corpach Pier was situated just outside the sea-lock and, to save time, a coach conveyed passengers between the sea-going steamers that called there and the canal boats at Banavie Pier.

Thomas Telford played a central role in another major transport undertaking through Corpach. He had been appointed as engineer to the Commissioners for Highland Roads and Bridges, a government body whose remit was to develop a road network throughout the Highlands. Telford identified routes and drew up specifications for contractors who were appointed to build the individual roads. Of the many routes to be built, the first was begun in 1804, running between Fort William and Arisaig, by way of the River Lochy ferry, the bridge over the Banavie canal locks and Corpach. The village grew up around both the canal and the road, which is seen here early in the twentieth century. Prior to these developments, and a little to the west, a community had become established alongside the Kilmallie Parish Church, placing Corpach at the heart of what was once the largest parish, by area, in Scotland. Built in 1783 on or near the site of at least two earlier churches, the church building was over twenty years old when the road builders were working their way past it.

Achdalieu House was built in 1885 on Loch Eil side, to the west of Corpach, as a shooting lodge. When it ceased to be used for that, and the local wildlife breathed a sigh of relief, it was put to a number of other uses including as a Second World War commando training base, a Christian residential centre and a hotel, before becoming an outward bound centre. Achdalieu was etched into the history of Fort William within days of the Cromwellian garrison arriving to establish Inverlochy Fort. A foraging party of soldiers was ashore when Cameron clansmen caught them by surprise. Although outnumbered, the Camerons, with their finely honed close-quarter, hand-to-hand fighting skills routed the soldiers, killing over sixty. It was a victory, but the timing wasn't great. General Monck, Cromwell's commander-in-chief in Scotland, was on manoeuvres near the head of Loch Lochy a few days later, and when he heard the news, ordered his men to burn houses as they passed through Cameron lands. It was a bloodless, but effective way of keeping the peace because men who had to re-build houses were not able to go looking for a fight.